Unto Us

25 Advent Devotions about the Messiah

EDITED *by*

WINFREE BRISLEY & JARED KENNEDY

Contents

Contributors

WINFREE BRISLEY serves as an editor for The Gospel Coalition. She is a Bible teacher and contributor to *The Weary World Rejoices: Daily Devotions for Advent* and *Fruitful: Cultivating a Spiritual Harvest That Won't Leave You Empty*. Winfree and her husband, Will, have three sons and live in Charlotte, North Carolina, where they belong to Uptown Church.

ELLIOT CLARK is an associate editor at The Gospel Coalition. He serves in international ministry, equipping church leaders and supporting residential missionaries. He is the author of *Evangelism as Exiles: Life on Mission as Strangers in Our Own Land* and *Mission Affirmed: Recovering the Missionary Motivation of Paul* and coeditor of *Faithful Exiles: Finding Hope in a Hostile World*.

SHARONDA COOPER (MEng, Massachusetts Institute of Technology) is a Bible teacher who serves as content coordinator for women's initiatives at The Gospel Coalition and is a contributor to *Fruitful: Cultivating a Spiritual Harvest That Won't Leave You Empty*. She is working toward her MDiv from The Southern Baptist Theological Seminary. She is a wife and mom, and she belongs to Emmaus Church in Texas.

KENDRA DAHL (MA, Westminster Seminary California) is the multimedia strategist for The Gospel Coalition. She is the author of *How to Keep Your Faith After High School* and several articles. She lives in the San Diego area with her husband and three children, where she also serves as the women's ministry coordinator for North Park Presbyterian Church.

BENJAMIN L. GLADD (PhD, Wheaton College) serves on The Gospel Coalition's staff as executive director of The Carson Center for Theological Renewal. He has authored and edited numerous books including *From Adam and Israel to the Church*, *Handbook on the Gospels*, *The Story Retold* (with G. K. Beale), and *Dictionary of the New Testament Use of the Old Testament* (with Beale, D. A. Carson, and Andrew David Naselli). He is also the editor of the Essential Studies in Biblical Theology series and coeditor with Carson of the New Studies in Biblical Theology series. Benjamin and his wife, Nikki, have two sons, Judah and Simon.

COLLIN HANSEN serves as vice president for content and editor in chief of The Gospel Coalition, as well as executive director of The Keller Center for Cultural Apologetics. He hosts the *Gospelbound* podcast and has written and contributed to many books, most recently *Timothy Keller: His Spiritual and Intellectual Formation* and *Rediscover Church: Why the Body of Christ Is Essential*. He is an adjunct professor at Beeson Divinity School, where he also cochairs the advisory board.

MEGAN HILL serves as the managing editor for The Gospel Coalition. She is the author of several books, including *Sighing on Sunday: 40 Meditations for When Church Hurts*. She lives with her husband and four children in Massachusetts, where they belong to West Springfield Covenant Community Church.

BETSY CHILDS HOWARD is an editor for The Gospel Coalition. She is the author of *Seasons of Waiting: Walking by Faith When Dreams Are Delayed* and the children's books *Arlo and the Great Big Cover-Up*, *Polly and the Screen Time Overload*, and *Arlo and the Keep-Out Club*. Betsy and her husband, Bernard, live with their two sons in Birmingham, Alabama, where Bernard is the pastor of Grace Church Birmingham.

JARED KENNEDY serves as an editor for The Gospel Coalition. He is editor for the TGC Hard Questions series and the author of books including *Keeping Your Children's Ministry on Mission*, *The Beginner's Gospel Story Bible*, and *The Story of Martin Luther*. He and his wife, Megan, live with their three daughters in Louisville, Kentucky, where they belong to Sojourn Church Midtown.

JOANNA KIMBREL (MATS, Westminster Theological Seminary) is a Bible teacher, a writer, and the coordinator of women's initiatives for The Gospel Coalition. She is coauthor of *Behold and Believe: A Bible Study on the "I Am" Statements of Jesus* and author of *The Greatest Hero: The Book of Romans*. Joanna and her husband, Chad, live in Georgia with their three daughters.

BRETT MCCRACKEN is a senior editor and director of communications at The Gospel Coalition. He is the author of several books, including *The Wisdom Pyramid: Feeding Your Soul in a Post-Truth World* and *Uncomfortable: The Awkward and Essential Challenge of Christian Community*. Brett and his wife, Kira, live in Santa Ana, California, with their three children. They belong to Southlands Church.

IVAN MESA (PhD candidate, The Southern Baptist Theological Seminary) is editorial director for The Gospel Coalition. He's editor of *Before You Lose Your Faith: Deconstructing Doubt in the Church* and coeditor of *Faithful Exiles: Finding Hope in a Hostile World*. He and his wife, Sarah, have four children, and they live in eastern Georgia.

MATT SMETHURST is lead pastor of River City Baptist Church in Richmond, Virginia; editor at The Gospel Coalition; and author of *Before You Open Your Bible*, *Before You Share Your Faith*, and *Deacons*. He and his wife, Maghan, have five children.

ANDREW SPENCER (PhD, Southeastern Baptist Theological Seminary) serves as associate editor for books at The Gospel Coalition. He is the author of *Hope for God's Creation: Stewardship in an Age of Futility*. Spencer is an elder at CrossPointe Church. He and his wife, Jennifer, have three children and live in southeast Michigan.

PHIL THOMPSON serves as program director for The Gospel Coalition's Carson Center for Theological Renewal. He's a teaching pastor at Christ Fellowship

Eastside and an adjunct professor at Columbia International University. He and his wife, Laurel, live with their three daughters in Greenville, South Carolina.

CASSIE WATSON is copy editor and editorial project manager for The Gospel Coalition. She lives in Sydney, Australia, and belongs to Merrylands Anglican Church. She blogs at CassWatson.com.

SARAH EEKHOFF ZYLSTRA is senior writer for The Gospel Coalition. She's a coauthor of *Gospelbound: Living with Resolute Hope in an Anxious Age* and editor of *Social Sanity in an Insta World.* She lives with her husband and two sons in Kansas City, Missouri, where they belong to New City Church.

Introduction

Christmas is a paradox of longing and fulfillment for Christians. We sing "Come Thou Long Expected Jesus" on the very holiday that celebrates his incarnation. We know Christ has already come, yet we long for him to come again. In fact, the reality that God is with us fuels our longing for his second advent.

Throughout December, we look back at God's Old Testament promises to send the Messiah to save his people. Then we see in the Gospel accounts how he did exactly what he said he'd do, down to the last detail. So as we read Jesus's New Testament promise to come again, we eagerly await the final day when our rescue will be complete.

Or maybe we don't. Perhaps we're so distracted by the cares of daily life that we don't give much thought to Christ's return. Maybe we're so used to relying on ourselves that we don't feel our need for the Savior. Maybe our satisfaction with worldly treasures has dulled our longing for the better portion. How can we rekindle our longing for Christ this Advent season? How can we prepare for his return with expectant hope?

John the Baptist prepared God's people for the Messiah's first coming and announced his arrival. Were that job assigned to us today, we'd likely design a marketing strategy, implement a social media campaign, or line up a string of podcast interviews. But John's approach was simple: he bore witness. He proclaimed, "Behold, the Lamb of God!" (John 1:36). John exhorted others to take a good look at Jesus, to see he was the Promised One, the Messiah they'd been waiting for.

The results were astonishing: "The two disciples heard him say this, and they followed Jesus" (v. 37). Simply by beholding Jesus, they were compelled to follow him—and to invite others to follow him too. After spending time with Jesus, one of those disciples, Andrew, went and told his brother Simon Peter, "We have found the Messiah" (v. 41).

What drove these men to abandon all and follow? What compelled them to share the good news with others? Meeting Jesus—the Son born *unto us* to be our Wonderful Counselor, Mighty God, Everlasting Father, and Prince of Peace (Isa. 9:6).

Whether we're entering this Advent season distracted or weary, anxious or doubting, hoping or hurting, we need to take a good look at Jesus. We need to remember he is the Messiah who came and is coming again. In Christ, our longings are both satisfied and stirred.

HOW TO USE THIS DEVOTIONAL

To help us look to Christ this Advent season, The Gospel Coalition's staff has written devotions that reflect on the Scripture texts in the Christmas section of Handel's *Messiah*. You've likely heard the music of this well-known oratorio, particularly the famous "Hallelujah" chorus. But you may not realize all the lyrics are Scripture passages arranged to tell the story of Christ as the long-awaited Savior.

We've included 25 devotions so you can begin on December 1 and work through one reading per day until Christmas. Each devotion includes a brief Scripture reading, a devotional reflection, and questions for response. We encourage you to find a recording of Handel's *Messiah* and listen to the corresponding movement for each day.

You may choose to use this devotional individually, asking the Spirit to satisfy and stir your longing for Christ. But we also encourage you to consider, as the disciples did, who you can invite to behold Jesus along with you. These devotions can be used for family worship, with a group from your church, or with an unbelieving neighbor or friend.

However you use it, we pray this devotional will help you reflect on the wonder and glory not of a beautiful piece of music but of the Messiah it celebrates. May it stir in our hearts a longing to join our voices with that great multitude John describes in Revelation 19:6–7, which cries out,

> Hallelujah!
> For the Lord our God
>   the Almighty reigns.
> Let us rejoice and exult
>   and give him the glory.

Surely he alone is worthy of all glory and honor and praise. Join us as we meditate on the Messiah this Christmas season. May we remember with fresh wonder that a Savior has been born *unto us*.

Winfree Brisley

PART I

Salvation Promised

Exodus from Exile

JARED KENNEDY

READ

"Thus says the LORD,
    who makes a way in the sea,
    a path in the mighty waters,
who brings forth chariot and horse,
    army and warrior;
they lie down, they cannot rise,
    they are extinguished, quenched like a wick:
'Remember not the former things,
    nor consider the things of old.
Behold, I am doing a new thing;
    now it springs forth, do you not perceive it?
I will make a way in the wilderness
    and rivers in the desert.'" (Isa. 43:16–19)

REFLECT

As the calendar nears December, we pull the lights out of the garage and the boxes of decorations from the attic. We set up the tree, hang the stockings, and start the annual Advent countdown. We bookmark the holiday playlist, finish (or begin!) the shopping, and mark down all the party dates. But in our Christmas busyness, do we see how God is at work in our daily lives? Do we remember how he has been at work over the past year?

We can see God working in the past and present, but the prophet Isaiah also saw God at work in the future. He called his firstborn son Shear-jashub (Isa. 7:3), a name that means "a remnant will return." This name was a surprising choice. After all, when little Shear was born, God's people still lived in the promised land. Isaiah named his children (and wrote his prophecies) well before Judah's exile to Babylon. So, on the eighth day after Shear-jashub's birth, when the boy's name was announced at his dedication, Isaiah's Jerusalem neighbors must've thought, *Hmm. Return from where?*

The people couldn't see what God was doing. They were blind to his future purposes (6:9–10). But God gave the prophet faith to see the certainty of the Lord's plans. Isaiah knew both exile and return loomed on the horizon. The nation's neglect of God's law, their busy self-reliance, and their trust in military pacts with foreign powers would end in judgment. To Babylonian exile they would go. But then, just as certainly, the Redeemer would deliver his people again (43:14–15).

What would this future salvation be like? God's redemptive pattern for Judah's future had already been revealed in the past. When the Hebrew people suffered under Egyptian oppression, God made a way of escape through the sea (v. 16). Now, said Isaiah, God would build another highway in the wilderness (v. 19). At the exodus, the Lord snuffed out Pharaoh's army with their chariots and horses (v. 17). Now, God would again do away with the people's worldly securities so they'd put their trust in him alone.

"Remember not the former things, nor consider the things of old," said the Lord. "Behold, I am doing a new thing" (vv. 18–19). If only the people could perceive it, they'd see God at work bringing forth his life-giving water (vv. 19–20). Though God's judgment still lay ahead, Isaiah also saw the day when sin would be atoned for and God's perfected people would declare his praise (v. 21).

God is still at work bringing new life today. In Christ, "the old has passed away; behold, the new has come" (2 Cor. 5:17). Do you see it? Just look back at what he's already done. At the cross, our incarnate Lord took the fullness of God's wrath for our rebellion and gave us his perfect record instead (Isa. 43:25). When we were dead in our transgressions, God made us alive by his Spirit (Eph. 2:1–10). Looking forward with faith, we await Christ's second coming as the final exodus and the fulfillment of all God's promises. We can trust God will work in the future just as he has in the past. He's doing a new thing. May we have eyes to see it.

RESPOND

As you begin this new holiday season, set aside time to remember Christ's work in your life. What has the Lord

done for you this past year? Did he answer a prayer?
Did he bring a friend or family member to faith? Give
God praise for the ways you've seen him work, and
pray with expectant hope for his continued work in the
coming year.

Comfort Ye My People

ANDREW SPENCER

READ

"Comfort, comfort my people, says your God.
Speak tenderly to Jerusalem,
    and cry to her
that her warfare is ended,
    that her iniquity is pardoned,
that she has received from the LORD's hand
    double for all her sins." (Isa. 40:1–2)

REFLECT

Most of us live relatively comfortable lives. Our houses are climate controlled; our pantries are full; we aren't overwhelmingly concerned about foreign invasions. It can be easy to forget what real physical discomfort feels

like. Yet many of us experience spiritual and psycholog-
ical discomfort from the pains of the world. Whatever
the source of our suffering, Isaiah has good news for
us—a Comforter has come and is coming again.

Today's verses from Isaiah are a reminder of God's
goodness toward his people. God had promised Hezeki-
ah in the previous chapter that they'd have a few more
years of freedom but then God's people would be overwhelmed by the Babylonians. God provided a glimpse of
hope amid the agony and dread. He wouldn't stop the
invasion. He would, however, ensure all would be well.
It was an incomplete comfort that anticipated a greater
comfort to come.

In our moments of greatest distress, we need someone to remind us things are going to be OK. When we
don't get the job we were hoping for, we need a friend
to remind us there will be other opportunities. When
medical bills pile up, we need someone to remind us we
have time to work out a plan. It doesn't take away all the
distress, but it does help us endure. More significantly,
when we look beyond our temporary discomforts and toward our spiritual freedom in Christ, it can help us bear
up under a mountain of bad news. *God is for us, our sin has
been pardoned, and it's going to be alright.* That's God's message to his people in this passage.

But even when words of comfort feel like a blanket
that doesn't quite cover our toes, the incomplete comfort
is a blessing because it reminds us of the greater comfort
to come. Isaiah predicted judgment was coming, but he
also reminded God's people that relief from judgment
would come. God doesn't promise us an easy life, but he
does promise complete renewal one day. We celebrate

the King's birth to remind us we still wait for the King's final coming. In Christ, our sins have been pardoned, and one day, the difficulties of this life will pass away.

When the night is darkest and our toes are coldest, we need a reminder this isn't the way life is supposed to be. Christmas is that reminder. The Advent season testifies that our sins have been paid for and the best days are ahead. We already know salvation is coming, yet we won't get the full measure of comfort until we see Christ face to face. There's comfort in that knowledge, even as we wait for the promise's fulfillment.

RESPOND

What burdens are you carrying this Advent season? How does it encourage you to remember that God's complete comfort is still to come?

Every Valley Shall Be Exalted

BETSY CHILDS HOWARD

READ

"A voice cries:
'In the wilderness prepare the way of the LORD;
     make straight in the desert a highway for our God.
Every valley shall be lifted up,
     and every mountain and hill be made low;
the uneven ground shall become level,
     and the rough places a plain.'" (Isa. 40:3–4)

REFLECT

It was said of Queen Elizabeth II that she must have thought the whole world smelled of fresh paint. When a monarch comes to visit, people prepare. The crack in the sidewalk that pedestrians have stumbled over for years will be smoothed and the potholes filled. It's not that the queen had more trouble walking than commoners or that a Rolls-Royce couldn't handle potholes. Rather, preparation is a way to show honor.

In the Gospels, we learn that the messenger prophesied by Isaiah, sent by God to prepare the way for the King of kings, was John the Baptist. John's preparation didn't involve any of the external sprucing up one would expect for a monarch's visit. Instead, he preached repentance for the forgiveness of sins. People who heard him were moved to confess their sins and be baptized. His message prepared their hearts, not their outward appearances.

The season of Advent helps us remember that not only has the Messiah come but he will come again. In his last recorded words, Jesus said, "Surely I am coming soon" (Rev. 22:20). We don't know the day or the hour, but we need to be prepared. So how should we prepare ourselves for Christ's return?

John the Baptist's call to repentance and forgiveness is still valid today as we wait for Jesus's second coming: "Repent, for the kingdom of heaven is at hand" (Matt. 3:2). Yet repentance isn't easy. C. S. Lewis writes,

> Fallen man is not simply an imperfect creature who needs improvement: he is a rebel who must lay down his arms. Laying down your arms, surrendering, saying you are sorry, realising that you have been on the wrong track and getting ready to start life over again from the ground floor . . . is what Christians call repentance. Now repentance is no fun at all. It is something much harder than merely eating humble pie. It means unlearning all the self-conceit and

self-will that we have been training ourselves into for thousands of years. It means . . . undergoing a kind of death.[1]

Repentance may be a kind of death, but it leads us to new life. The heart of the Christian faith isn't making ourselves look better on the outside but having God truly cleanse our hearts.

All the fresh paint in the world won't make us ready for Jesus. We'll only be ready when we acknowledge ourselves as sinners in need of the Savior. As one hymn puts it,

> Come, ye thirsty, come, and welcome,
> God's free bounty glorify;
> true belief and true repentance,
> every grace that brings you nigh.
>
> Let not conscience make you linger,
> nor of fitness fondly dream;
> all the fitness He requireth
> is to feel your need of Him.[2]

Do you feel your need of Jesus? He is ready and willing to save all who put their trust in him. Come, Lord Jesus!

1. C. S. Lewis, *Mere Christianity* (1952; repr., London: William Collins, 2016), 56–57.
2. Joseph Hart, "Come Ye Sinners, Poor and Needy" (1759), Hymnary.org, accessed April 10, 2024, https://hymnary.org/text/come_ye_sinners_poor_and_needy_weak_and.

RESPOND

Ask the Lord to search your heart. Is there sin in your life that makes you hope Christ will delay his return? What would repentance from this sin look like? Pray that God would once again make straight the way for his Son to appear, bringing the fullness of his kingdom.

And the Glory of the Lord Shall Be Revealed

CASSIE WATSON

READ

"And the glory of the LORD shall be revealed,
    and all flesh shall see it together,
        for the mouth of the LORD has spoken." (Isa. 40:5)

REFLECT

To say I'm bossy about Christmas is an understatement.

As a kid, I insisted my sisters and I sleep in the same bedroom on Christmas Eve so we could all enter the living room together in the morning and share the first sight of presents piled under the tree. I made sure they both had a water bottle and a book to read if they woke up early, so they wouldn't need to venture out and ruin the wonder. (As an adult, I've tried to convince them to ditch their husbands for a night so we can keep the tradition going. No luck so far.)

Glory abounds at Christmas—in that sight of presents under the tree, in spectacular light displays, in the rousing harmonies of a congregation singing carols by candlelight. If we're not careful, we become captivated by the wonder of all the secondary glories of Christmas and miss the main event.

Isaiah knew what it meant to behold true glory. He was given a vision of God on his throne, and it almost killed him: "Woe is me! For I am lost; for I am a man of unclean lips, and I dwell in the midst of a people of unclean lips; for my eyes have seen the King, the LORD of hosts!" (Isa. 6:5).

Yet Isaiah wasn't the only one who'd get to see the Lord. Through the prophet's words, God comforted his people exiled in Babylon with an astonishing promise: "The glory of the LORD shall be revealed, and all flesh shall see it together" (40:5).

At Christmastime, we celebrate the coming of this glory. Jesus took on humanity, and he entered our world in a grubby stable. Glory arrived. "The Word became flesh and dwelt among us, and we have seen his glory, glory as of the only Son from the Father, full of grace and truth" (John 1:14).

Most who saw Jesus during his lifetime missed his glory. But now, in the Bible, we see it—the glory of his miracles; his teaching; his sinlessness; his death, resurrection, and ascension. Do you see it? Or are your eyes fixed on something else this Christmas?

Amid the festive spectacles, are you too distracted to look on and bask in the glory of your Savior? Do your eyes flit so quickly between your calendar, your to-do list, and your messy house that you don't even notice Christ?

Through Scripture, we behold Jesus now. As we look, the Spirit transforms us more and more into Jesus's image so we share his glory (2 Cor. 3:18). Yet this isn't enough. Charles Spurgeon wrote, "How partially we see Christ here. The best believer only gets half a glimpse of Christ."[1]

These partial glimpses make us long for Christ's return, when we'll finally see him face to face. Only then will Isaiah's prophecy be fulfilled as God keeps his promise: "The glory of the LORD shall be revealed, and all flesh shall see it together, for the mouth of the LORD has spoken."

On that day, we'll delight together at the greatest spectacle any of us has ever seen. In anticipation of that glory, we can rejoice in what Scripture reveals of Jesus today. Let's look and look until we see.

RESPOND

Who or what has most of your attention this Christmas? What habits or practices can you start in the coming weeks to fix your eyes on Christ's glory? How might you stir your longing for his return amid the season's busyness?

---

1. Charles Haddon Spurgeon, "The Beatific Vision," a sermon preached at the Metropolitan Tabernacle on January 20, 1856, https://www. spurgeon.org/resource-library/sermons/the-beatific-vision/.

PART II

God Comes

Yet Once More
I Will Shake

COLLIN HANSEN

READ

"For thus says the LORD of hosts: Yet once more, in a little while, I will shake the heavens and the earth and the sea and the dry land. And I will shake all nations, so that the treasures of all nations shall come in, and I will fill this house with glory, says the LORD of hosts." (Hag. 2:6–7)

REFLECT

When this prophecy came to Haggai in 520 BC, did anyone imagine that God would shake up the world with a baby born to humble parents in Bethlehem? Or that "a little while" would be more than 500 years later?

Yet if Advent teaches us anything, it's that the Lord works according to his own schedule and doesn't act as we expect. His timeline may not align with ours, but in the passage of centuries we experience his mercy. We read in 2 Peter 3:9, "The Lord is not slow to fulfill his promise as some count slowness, but is patient toward you, not wishing that any should perish, but that all should reach repentance."

In Hebrews 12:26, the writer expands on this relationship between patience and judgment by quoting Haggai 2. The shaking is a kind of sifting, like the sand separated from jewels in a strainer. The Lord shakes the world to sift out anyone who doesn't worship that baby born in Bethlehem. Because even as a helpless babe, he is the King of kings and Lord of lords who will reign forever. In Jesus we see "the radiance of the glory of God and the exact imprint of his nature," the One who "upholds the universe by the word of his power" (Heb. 1:3).

One day, after a little while, that baby would grow up and exercise his power in the most unexpected way. He would submit to death, even on a cross. The day he died on Calvary, the temple curtain was torn in two. An earthquake shook the city. Rocks split at the Place of a Skull (Matt. 27:32, 51). That helpless man, bloodied and beaten, commanded more authority than anyone else had realized—including the power to judge his judges. The Roman officer who commanded 100 confessed, "Truly this was the Son of God!" (v. 54).

Those who don't follow suit will be sifted. But the shed blood of the only Son of God has the power to forgive the sins of all who repent. By this sacrifice, believers will receive a "kingdom that cannot be shaken" (Heb. 12:28).

To this kingdom all the treasures of the nations will accrue, as Haggai foresaw with the temple filled by God's glory. God did this for the Hebrews when he delivered them from slavery. They plundered the Egyptians (Ex. 12:36). And he'll do it again when he delivers the world from death, as the kings of the earth bring their glory to the temple in the new Jerusalem (Rev. 21:24).

These kings will follow a path already trod by the wise men of the east, who tracked the star to baby Jesus. From the nations they brought their treasures—gold, frankincense, and myrrh. The purported king, Herod, could only see a threat. But these wise men fell down and worshiped the baby still nursing with his mother, Mary (Matt. 2:11).

Do you see the power and the glory concealed from the world while contained in that baby? Do you see in him a King whose love for sinners kept him nailed to the cross?

Advent is waiting for something that not everyone can see. Advent is preparing to receive a gift that not everyone wants. Advent is enduring an unstable world with hope because an unshakable kingdom is coming— in a little while.

RESPOND

How might the Lord's seeming lack of action express his patience for you? How could you help your non-Christian friends and family see the glory in Jesus this Advent season?

The Lord You Seek Will Suddenly Come

MEGAN HILL

READ

"Behold, I send my messenger, and he will prepare the way before me. And the Lord whom you seek will suddenly come to his temple; and the messenger of the covenant in whom you delight, behold, he is coming, says the LORD of hosts." (Mal. 3:1)

REFLECT

When I'm baking holiday treats, one of my kids will usually ask for a taste—a lick of frosting, a corner of crumbled cake, a dab of chocolate batter. Inevitably, just as he pops the last bit in his mouth, another child appears in the kitchen, demanding to know why *he* wasn't offered a sample. "Well," I always say, "your brother was in the right place at the right time." I love it when my kids hang out where I am, and I make sure they all know spending time with me is the surest route to extra Christmas cookies.

In today's verse, God's Old Testament people heard a similar message: to behold the Messiah, you need to be in the right place at the right time.

Over the 400 years following Malachi's prophecy, some of God's people lost heart and lost focus. But a faithful remnant remained. Luke 2 tells the story of one of them, a woman named Anna. Anna believed Malachi's words that God would send the Promised One and that he'd show up in the temple. So Anna "did not depart from the temple, worshiping with fasting and prayer night and day" (v. 37). When the Messiah came, however suddenly, Anna wasn't going to miss it for the world.

And the Lord fulfilled his promise. Anna was likely there on the day Zechariah stumbled, mute, out of the holy place with the seed of the messenger in his body and the promise of the messenger's mission in his heart (1:5–23). And she was there when Mary and Joseph finally walked through the gates with the newborn Savior in their arms (2:22, 27, 38). After seeking the Lord for a lifetime, Anna was ready with eyes of faith to witness his appearing.

Malachi's words were the last revelation God's people received before centuries of prophetic silence, but this verse assured the faithful that preparations for the Messiah's coming were underway and encouraged them to be ready. In our day we, too, have the promise of Christ's appearing—if we're in the right place at the right time.

Christ promises to be with us when we gather with his church (Matt. 18:18–20; Heb. 2:11–12). He

promises to manifest himself as we love him and one another (John 14:21; 1 John 4:12–13). He promises to indwell
us and teach us by his Spirit as we walk in obedience to
his Word (John 14:15–24). He promises to accompany us
as we take his gospel to the nations (Matt. 28:18–20). If
we want to encounter the Messiah, we have only to seek
him in the places he says he'll be found.

We also have a promise that Christ will again appear
in the flesh—"Surely I am coming soon"(Rev. 22:20)—not
announced by a single messenger but by every member
of his worldwide church, not in a man-made temple in
Jerusalem but in the heavenly gathering of his people,
not as a baby but as a triumphant King.

Are you ready?

RESPOND

What activity or event are you looking forward to this
holiday season? How will you make sure you don't miss
it? How does today's verse help you prepare to encounter Jesus? What's one thing you can do this week to
make sure you're in the right place at the right time to
behold him?

Who May Abide the Day of His Coming?

ELLIOT CLARK

READ

"But who can endure the day of his coming, and who can stand when he appears? For he is like a refiner's fire and like fullers' soap." (Mal. 3:2)

REFLECT

Not many Christmas carols reference soap and fire. Of course, there are plenty of seasonal tunes that celebrate hearth and home, close friends and a fire's glow, even chestnuts over an open flame. But mention of a smelting furnace and a scouring detergent seems out of place in a holiday hymn—maybe even in an Advent devotional. That's because we associate Christmas with joy and peace, not judgment and purification.

Yet Malachi offers another perspective. When he predicts the Lord's coming, he doesn't give us images of an infant meek and mild. No. He's like a refiner's fire. He's like fullers' soap. Abrasive. Harsh. Extreme. Hot. And who can abide the day of his coming?

Malachi isn't the only Old Testament author to ask this question (Nah. 1:6; Ps. 76:7). When the prophets foretell the Lord's coming—often referred to as "the day of the Lord"—they speak of retribution. It will be a great and terrible day. A day of thick darkness. A day of reckoning. The final words of Malachi's prophecy—the very last words of our Old Testament—predict the day of the Lord will come with "utter destruction" (Mal. 4:6).

This explains John the Baptist's opening line in the Gospels. The New Testament begins with John preparing the way of the Lord in fulfillment of Malachi's prophecy. When John announces the arrival of the King, he warns of coming devastation. Fruitless branches will meet flames. Useless chaff will burn. The One coming will baptize with fire (Luke 3:1–17). Therefore, John calls the crowds to repent.

Repentance is the only appropriate response to news of the Lord's coming. Otherwise, as Malachi's rhetorical question implies, you won't be able to endure. No one can stand before the refiner's fire and the fuller's soap. And when you know you can't stand, it's best to get on your knees.

This may not be a message we typically hear at Christmastime. But it's a necessary word. Without confession, who can abide the day of the Lord?

During the Advent season, we're right to celebrate the angels' message of goodwill toward men and peace on earth. We're right to worship with songs of joy and mirth. Because, in the mystery of grace, Jesus's first advent wasn't marked by condemnation but compassion. He came in mercy rather than wrath.

Yet such mercy is only possible because the baby in the manger would one day bear God's fiery judgment in our place. The spotless Lamb would willingly lay down his life, making purification for sins. In the words of an old hymn, we're saved from wrath and made pure—a double cure.[1]

This is the wonder of the gospel: Christ was cursed so we could be clean. We're washed white in his precious blood. At the cross, soap and fire come together for our salvation.

RESPOND

Is confession of sin and repentance a regular part of your Advent traditions? Take a moment to acknowledge your guilt before God and thank him for his amazing grace to you in Christ.

---

1. Augustus Toplady, "Rock of Ages" (1776), Hymnary.org, accessed April 10, 2024, https://hymnary.org/text/rock_of_ages_cleft_for_me_let_me_hide.

And He Shall Purify

SHARONDA COOPER

READ

"He will sit as a refiner and purifier of silver, and he will purify the sons of Levi and refine them like gold and silver, and they will bring offerings in righteousness to the LORD. Then the offering of Judah and Jerusalem will be pleasing to the LORD as in the days of old and as in former years." (Mal. 3:3–4)

REFLECT

My grandmother always made going to church a special event. She helped me pick the right dress, made sure my shoes were shiny and clean, and withstood burns from the curling iron to perfect my hairdo. I know church attire can vary. But I still get dressed up for corporate worship because, no matter how cliché it sounds, I want to wear my Sunday best for Jesus.

Yet even in our finest clothes, we can still be dirty on the inside. Hidden sins are, after all, *hidden*. We can sing hymns at max volume, forgetting the way we treated our coworkers last week. We can kneel in prayer, easily dismissing what we posted on the internet earlier that morning. We can take the bread and wine even if we lost it with our kids in the car. People at church only see what's on the outside, but God looks on the heart (1 Sam. 16:7). And unless we come clean, we can't come into his presence at all.

Purity in God's presence is a major theme in Scripture. In Leviticus, we learn how Israel was to distinguish between the clean and unclean. These categories extended to foods and animals. Even people could be defiled by disease or by touching unclean things such as a dead body. The temple was off-limits for the unclean. Only ritual washings and animal sacrifices made reentry into God's presence achievable. But even this wasn't permanent—for the blood of bulls and goats couldn't fully atone for sin (Heb. 10:4).

Like Israel, we dare not present ourselves before God in our sinful condition. As the psalmist asks, "Who shall stand in [God's] holy place? He who has clean hands and a pure heart" (Ps. 24:3–4). While soap and water might wash our filthy hands, what can purify our sin-stained hearts?

In today's verses, the prophet Malachi announced the coming of One who would refine his people as gold and silver. Later, the author of Hebrews clarified the refiner's identity:

If the blood of goats and bulls . . . sanctify for the purification of the flesh, how much more will the blood of Christ, who through the eternal Spirit offered himself without blemish to God, purify our conscience from dead works to serve the living God. (Heb. 9:13–14)

During Advent, we remember that Jesus is the great Refiner. He came to shed his purifying blood to cover our sins and forgive us. Then, like a refiner who heats metal to remove impurities, the Lord sanctifies us so that on judgment day we'll be an unblemished offering to God. On that day, because of Jesus, we'll wear white robes of righteousness (Rev. 6:11).

Grandma made sure I looked pretty for church, but I wasn't truly clean. Jesus, the great Purifier of sinners, is the only One who can wash away every stain and remove every impurity. When he dresses us in white robes, we'll enter God's presence because we'll be clean—not just on the outside but on the inside too.

RESPOND

Sometimes the Lord refines us through trials and difficult circumstances. How have you experienced his refining process this year? Write a prayer thanking God for Christ who cleanses, purifies, and refines us so we'll one day be holy and acceptable in his presence.

PART III

Light Comes

A Virgin Shall Conceive

CASSIE WATSON

READ

"Therefore the Lord himself will give you a sign. Behold, the virgin shall conceive and bear a son, and shall call his name Immanuel." (Isa. 7:14)

REFLECT

If you watch even a few holiday movies this year, you'll encounter the trope of the "Christmas miracle." The festive season apparently has the magical ability to bring soulmates together, rescue floundering family businesses, and heal incurable diseases.

The impossible becomes possible when December 25 rolls around.

The nation of Judah in Isaiah's day was in dire need of a miracle. They were in a centuries-long cycle of sin and rebellion against God. The northern kingdom of

Israel had joined forces with Syria, and together they threatened to attack. Judah's evil king, Ahaz, wouldn't submit to God. What hope did they have?

Despite Ahaz's hard-heartedness, God shows grace by making a promise: "The Lord himself will give you a sign. Behold, the virgin shall conceive and bear a son, and shall call his name Immanuel" (Isa. 7:14). Later, in Matthew's Gospel, we learn that "Immanuel" means "God with us" (Matt. 1:23). A spark of light appears in Judah's dark future. But it didn't seem like it could happen. A virgin bearing a son? Impossible. God dwelling among sinful people? Impossible.

Yet this is what we celebrate at Christmas. Matthew recounts Jesus's birth and tells us that "all this took place to fulfill what the Lord had spoken by the prophet" (v. 22)—Christ is the ultimate fulfillment of God's promise through Isaiah. God did the impossible.

What seems impossible to you this Christmas? You may have a list of tasks, commitments, and events so long that you can't possibly get it all done—let alone with a sense of peace, contentment, or even sanity. You may be facing family conflict, and you don't know how to begin healing the divides. You may be grieving, and the prospect of finding any holiday joy seems remote.

God doesn't promise to do everything that seems impossible. On Christmas morning, we won't find all our struggles tied up with a neat bow like the gifts under our trees. But God, our Immanuel, will be with us through it all. Impossible as it once seemed, God himself "came into the world to save sinners" (1 Tim. 1:15). He's with us now by his Spirit, and one day he'll return to make a new world and dwell with us physically and eternally.

So this Advent season, look to your God who does the impossible. Pray earnestly for peace and rest, for healing, for reconciliation, for joy. But remember he has already given us what we need. He's redefined what's impossible: "Neither death nor life, nor angels nor rulers, nor things present nor things to come, nor powers, nor height nor depth, nor anything else in all creation, will be able to separate us from the love of God in Christ Jesus our Lord" (Rom. 8:38–39). It's impossible that he'll abandon us.

Because God is steadfastly with us, we can face what seems insurmountable this Christmas. Our weaknesses and sins will not hinder God's determination to save and dwell among his people. He is God with us, now and forever, as the apostle John sees in his vision of the future: "Behold, the dwelling place of God is with man. He will dwell with them, and they will be his people, and God himself will be with them as their God" (Rev. 21:3).

RESPOND

What impossible situation are you facing this Christmas? Spend time praying about that today. Consider what we learn about the Lord from these verses and how that changes the way you think about your struggles or fears. What difference does it make that God is with you?

Good Tidings to Zion

SARAH EEKHOFF ZYLSTRA

READ

"Go on up to a high mountain,
 O Zion, herald of good news;
lift up your voice with strength,
 O Jerusalem, herald of good news;
 lift it up, fear not;
say to the cities of Judah,
 'Behold your God!'" (Isa. 40:9)

REFLECT

When I first started writing for The Gospel Coalition, my editor told me we were going to report good news. We were going to tell stories of where Christians were helping and the kingdom was advancing. We were going to say, "Behold, church, how God is at work in the world!"

Neither of us had a lot of confidence it'd work. We have education and experience in journalism, and we know there's a reason joy, peace, and cooperation aren't often featured in articles. Nobody reads those stories.

That's not because humans are insensitive monsters. It's because when we read bad news, our bodies react with fight or flight instincts—studies show our hearts beat faster and our skin begins to perspire.[1] We want to understand or process what's going on, so we click on the link and read past the headline.

When we read good news, on the other hand, we have no physiological response. Heart rates and perspiration levels stay the same. Researchers say it's the same nonresponse we have when we look at a blank screen.

For a long time, I was frustrated with God for creating us this way. Why didn't he make us able to absorb bad news calmly and react to good news with wild, enthusiastic joy? Wouldn't that be better? Wouldn't that make Isaiah's job easier? And John the Baptist's? And Jesus's? Wouldn't that make the church's job easier?

"Behold your God!" we could say to the world. "Isn't he amazing? Isn't it wonderful what he has done for us?" And the secular world would shout back, "Hooray! Praise the Lord!"

But that's not how God did it. And only recently did I begin to spot the beauty in his way.

1. Stuart Soroka, Patrick Fournier, and Lilach Nir, "Cross-National Evidence of a Negativity Bias in Psychophysiological Reaction to News," *Proceedings of the National Academy of Sciences* 116, no. 38 (September 2019): 18888–92, https://doi.org/10.1073/pnas.1908369116.

First, it's right that human bodies react with stress and anxiety to news of sin and brokenness in the world. That's a sign we were made for another world, one that isn't steeped in corruption and sadness. It's a testimony that God himself, the One we image, doesn't ignore evil. The tension we feel is a tiny shadow of God's reaction when he sees depravity unfolding across space and time.

Second, just because we stay relaxed when reading good reports or stories doesn't mean we're unaffected. Studies show that when we hear positive news, we're not only happier but more likely to take action[2]—to respond with compassion and energy to the world around us.[3]

There's no better news than the gospel—the message that God sent his Son to die on a cross for our sins and open a way for us to be reconciled to him. Our good God offers us not only salvation from our past but purpose for our present and hope for our future.

This good news changed, and continues to change, the world. Out of grateful joy, Christians have become missionaries, started schools, and adopted children. They've moved to broken places, given away their time and money, and forgiven those who sinned against them. They've preached the gospel, made countercultural choices, and kept doggedly working long before they saw any fruit.

2.   "The Motivational Power of Positive News Stories," University of Southampton, May 15, 2023, https://www.southampton.ac.uk/research/highlights/the-motivational-power-of-positive-news-stories.
3.   Sydney Page, "Stories of Kindness Can Ease the Angst of Upsetting News, Study Says," *Washington Post*, June 13, 2023, https://www.washingtonpost.com/lifestyle/2023/06/13/good-news-positivity-helps-distress/.

Behold, our God! What marvelous things he has done in us, is doing through us, and has planned for us.

RESPOND

Consider your news diet. If good news energizes us, how can you limit your bad news intake or find more good news? How can you keep reminding yourself of the good news of the gospel?

Darkness Covers

BRETT MCCRACKEN

READ

"For behold, darkness shall cover the earth,
    and thick darkness the peoples;
but the LORD will arise upon you,
    and his glory will be seen upon you.
And nations shall come to your light,
    and kings to the brightness of your rising."
(Isa. 60:2–3)

REFLECT

There's something about a sunrise. It wakes the world. Unlike the jarring blare of an alarm clock, a sunrise quietly whispers "Wake, O sleeper" with the graceful love of a parent rubbing a sleeping child's back.

When the sun rises, the slumbering stir to life. We've just spent seven or eight hours dead to the world. Then the sunrise triggers in us what looks like a resurrection. We rise. Certain flowers—daisies, poppies, and the apt-ly named morning glories—open their blossoms at the sun's rising. Little by little, empty streets fill and quiet houses stir. Drawn to the warmth and energy of the just-unveiled sun, we transition from rest to work, stillness to activity.

It's not surprising that the sun is an oft-used metaphor for God. For he, too, resurrects the dead. He, too, is the Giver of life and growth. He, too, draws all things to himself—such as the trees, which by nature grow upward, toward the sun, their branches like arms raised in perpetual worship.

This is the created order. All things were made to be drawn to and sustained by the sun. We were made to be alive insofar as we live, grow, and flourish by solar energy. So too with God. We're in darkness and death without him. As he bestows his grace on us, we rise to new life. We're able to grow. Like the sunflower blossom, which turns to follow the sun wherever it's positioned in the sky, we're created to look to the Lord, who "will arise upon [us], and his glory will be seen upon [us]" (Isa. 60:2).

In a world of darkness, we ache for the light. We wait for the sunrise. All nations, all kings, all people share this in common. The horizon each of us looks to—the nature of the "new day" we await—may be different: A new job. A remodeled home. A regime change. But only the sunrise of Christ will eternally satisfy. His is "the true light, which gives light to everyone" (John 1:9). Isaiah's prophecy was fulfilled in him.

The general revelation of God's created order—darkness and light, night and day—primes every created thing to know they *need* light, a salvation from outside themselves. The special revelation of Christ reveals a truer light than even the sun: the light that is our eternal life, the light the darkness will never overcome (v. 5), the light that will one day end night as we know it (Rev. 22:5).

RESPOND

How is God's glory seen in your life? How are you reflecting his beauty? In contrast to those who dwell in darkness, how does your life reflect 1 Thessalonians 5:5: "You are all children of light, children of the day. We are not of the night or of the darkness"?

Light Appears

JOANNA KIMBREL

READ

"The people who walked in darkness
    have seen a great light;
those who dwelt in a land of deep darkness,
    on them has light shone." (Isa. 9:2)

"Arise, shine, for your light has come,
    and the glory of the LORD has risen upon you."
(Isa. 60:1)

REFLECT

When darkness surrounds us, it can feel as if light will never shine again. Darkness comes in many forms—the grief of disease and death and shattered dreams, the thick gloom of depression, the hatred and violence that characterizes the nightly news, the hurt from those closest to us, the oppression of our own sin. Darkness touches us all, and it's unrelenting.

We ask, *Will this darkness ever lift?* Advent answers with a resounding yes. Dawn will come after the night. Those who live in perpetual darkness will lift their eyes to see the sunrise breaking through, and it will shine on them with hope and healing and life.

The Israelites walked in darkness as they waited for the arrival of the promised Messiah who would bring peace and healing for their brokenness. He would save them from their enemies and their sin and give them access to God's glorious presence at last. They waited eagerly, over what I imagine felt like an agonizing period, for night to end. And then, centuries after Isaiah prophesied about the coming light, Jesus announced, "I am the light of the world. Whoever follows me will not walk in darkness, but will have the light of life" (John 8:12). The birth of Jesus marked the dawning of a great light.

Jesus is the light who took on our darkness. The world's sin and shame was laid on him like a thick cloak until death extinguished the light in his eyes. Still, the darkness couldn't overcome the light (1:5). Jesus rose, proving darkness doesn't have the final word in his life. By faith in Jesus, neither will it in ours.

The light of the world has come—hallelujah!—but the darkness isn't yet gone. We still sense its presence daily as we're harassed by the shadow of suffering and sin that threatens to engulf us. Yes, there's comfort and healing and life in Christ now, but it isn't complete. Just as the sunrise begins as a faint glow in the dark before bursting forth in full glory, so it is with Christ. The light has come and is coming.

During Advent, we remember how God's people waited for the birth of Christ, but we also wait for his second coming. When he returns, there'll be no hint of darkness. Jesus Christ will be the lamp that brings light to the whole world (Rev. 21:23).

So we take heart, because darkness will not always endure. On that day, we too will rise from the dead and shine with the glory of God. He will wipe away every tear from our eyes, and the second coming of the light will disperse the shadows forever—no more death, no more mourning, no more tears, no more pain (v. 4). No longer will we walk in deep darkness but in everlasting light.

RESPOND

What are some ways darkness affects you now? Think about your health, your sin, your fears. Now reimagine what those circumstances would look like if darkness were eradicated. How might thinking about Christ's second coming influence the way you navigate your circumstances?

INTERLUDE

Unto Us a Child Is Born

Wonderful Counselor

WINFREE BRISLEY

READ

"For to us a child is born,
    to us a son is given;
and the government shall be upon his shoulder,
    and his name shall be called
Wonderful Counselor." (Isa. 9:6)

REFLECT

When I was a child, making my Christmas list was easy. I could fill a page with things I wanted in no time. But the older I get, the harder it is to answer the question "What do you want for Christmas?" It's not just that I'm picky or that I already have more than I need, though both of those are probably true. It's that the things I want most aren't for sale. Like wisdom. I'd really love wisdom for Christmas this year.

Our culture seems to think there's an app, podcast, book, or influencer to solve all our problems. Struggling with work-life balance? Get this new time tracking app. Need parenting help? Listen to this podcast. Want more energy and a healthier lifestyle? Follow this social media influencer.

All these can be helpful to a degree. But I'm looking for more than life hacks. I'm looking for life-giving wisdom to help me faithfully steward my gifts and responsibilities.

I don't just want time management strategies; I want help discerning whether that work opportunity is a worthwhile use of my time or an unnecessary drain on my family. I don't just want trendy parenting tips; I want to know how to help my three sons flourish as the people God made them to be. I don't just want products and routines to help me fight aging; I want to know what it looks like to keep pouring myself out for the kingdom as my capacity changes.

The real questions that weigh on my heart and mind can't be answered with a Google search or YouTube video. And often, they're not directly answered in the Bible either. That's why we need wisdom. As Tim Keller often explained, in the majority of life situations, there's not a moral rule to apply—wisdom is knowing the right thing to do.[1]

I often wish God had given us more specific guidance in his Word. But he gave us something better than

---

1. Tim Keller, "The Wellspring of Wisdom," *Gospel in Life* (podcast), November 5, 2021, https://podcast.gospelinlife.com/e/the-wellspring-of-wisdom-1635522489/.

turn-by-turn instructions. He gave us his Son, whose name is Wonderful Counselor. Jesus "became to us wisdom from God" (1 Cor. 1:30). In him are "hidden all the treasures of wisdom and knowledge" (Col. 2:3).

Not knowing what to do drives us to the One who does. If I had detailed instructions for every circumstance of life, I could pretend I'm sufficient on my own. But because I'm daily confronted with situations where I'm not sure what it looks like to be a faithful servant, or a loving neighbor, or a bold witness, I keep coming back to the Wonderful Counselor, realizing my dependence on him. He doesn't only have wisdom; he gives it generously to those who lack it and ask him for it (James 1:5).

So go ahead and ask the Lord for wisdom this Christmas. It's a gift he delights to give. But as you do, remember that God's true gift to us isn't wisdom alone—it's a relationship with Wisdom himself. Jesus came to live among us and left his Spirit to live within us, not primarily because God wants us to know the wise thing to do in every situation but because he wants us to know him.

RESPOND

What are situations in your life where you need wisdom and counsel? How can you seek Christ as your Wonderful Counselor this week?

Mighty God

JARED KENNEDY

READ

"For to us a child is born,
    to us a son is given;
and the government shall be upon his shoulder,
    and his name shall be called
. . . Mighty God." (Isa. 9:6)

REFLECT

As Christmas approaches, we rightly think and sing about the lowly Christ child whose "sweet head" Mary laid down in the manger. With reverence, we reflect on his innocent humility, and it inspires visions of quiet holiness. "No crying he makes," the children's choir sings. We love the quiet baby Jesus, but his holy gentleness is only part of the story.

In Isaiah 9, amid one of the greatest predictions of
the Savior's birth, we find a different declaration. The
prophet tells us the Christ child will be a prince who car-
ries political power on his shoulders and the sword of jus-
tice at his side. Here the child is described as "Mighty."
Isaiah uses the same Hebrew word used to describe David's "mighty men" in 2 Samuel 23:8. The young prince
was born to be a warrior king.

Maybe militaristic language like this makes you uncomfortable. After all, didn't Jesus tell Peter to put away
his sword (Matt. 26:52)? Isn't the vision of Christ as a
fighter a misguided notion that puts Christians in danger
of reliving the Crusades? "We don't need a gun-toting,
cowboy Jesus," some will say.

It's true that at the first Christmas, "God did not
send his Son into the world to condemn the world, but
in order that the world might be saved through him"
(John 3:17). Even now, his church doesn't "wrestle against
flesh and blood, but against . . . the cosmic powers . . .
[and] the spiritual forces of evil in the heavenly places"
(Eph. 6:12). The "victory that has overcome the world" is
found not in a clenched fist but in "our faith" (1 John 5:4).
Yet it's the prophet's prediction that Jesus is a mighty
warrior that gives his church the strength to stay focused
on our good-news mission.

You see, Isaiah didn't merely say the coming child
would be a mighty prince. He declared the newborn
babe would be the Warrior God himself. This should
make us tremble, but it should also comfort us. In Isaiah
10 (the chapter that follows the "for to us" promise), Isaiah announces, "A remnant will return, the remnant of
Jacob, to the mighty God" (v. 21). Why does the believing

remnant find comfort in a Warrior God? Because he's the One who'll wield his sword against all the injustice they face in this world. He'll punish those who rob the poor and needy among his people. He'll vanquish all who practice iniquity (vv. 1–2).

Today, our culture sees human life as disposable. Our economic systems reward greed. Sexual purity and marital faithfulness are mocked. And our political leaders again and again prove powerless to effect lasting change. Where is our hope amid this brokenness and sin? It's in the strong shoulders of our Mighty God. At Christmas, we remember how Jesus came in humility to save us from our sinful participation in this world's injustices. But we also look forward to the day when our Warrior King will come again to punish every evildoer who remains in his or her sin. On that day, he will right every wrong. The gentle Savior born on Christmas will rescue his faithful remnant from all this world's oppression.

RESPOND

What injustices do you see in your community and our larger culture? How does Jesus's name "Mighty God" encourage you to trust him with the brokenness around you? Lift this brokenness and sin to the Lord in prayer.

Everlasting Father

SARAH EEKHOFF ZYLSTRA

READ

"For to us a child is born,
    to us a son is given;
and the government shall be upon his shoulder,
    and his name shall be called
. . . Everlasting Father." (Isa. 9:6)

REFLECT

When I was a high school freshman, my dad walked out of our house one morning and never walked back in.

Maybe your dad left too. Maybe he was never there to begin with. Maybe he divorced your mom. Maybe he was so terrible at being a father you wish he'd left. Maybe, like mine, he died.

The United States leads the world in rates of fatherless children—about a quarter of kids under 18 now live

in a house without their dad.[1] It's not ideal. Studies tell
us kids without a dad present in their lives are more likely to act out, quit school, and live in poverty.[2] They're
less likely to find stable jobs and more likely to use drugs
or go to jail. They're more likely to be depressed and anxious, even into adulthood.

Isaiah promised the coming child would be called
"Everlasting Father." But for many of us, that promise is
so far from our reality it's hard to picture. What would it
be like if your dad didn't leave? Didn't die? Didn't check
out mentally?

We can only know what it's like to have a perfect father because Christ promised to take on that role for us.
"I will not leave you as orphans; I will come to you," Jesus
says (John 14:18).

Christ doesn't only act like a loving father toward us;
he also brings us into his heavenly Father's family: "To all
who did receive [Jesus], who believed in his name, he gave
the right to become children of God, who were born, not
of blood nor of the will of the flesh nor of the will of man,
but of God" (1:12–13). John also wrote, "See what kind of
love the Father has given to us, that we should be called
children of God; and so we are" (1 John 3:1).

It's one of the most startling claims of the Bible—
that we could be God's kids. That we could look like him

1.   Stephanie Kramer, "U.S. Has World's Highest Rate of Children Living
     in Single-Parent Households," Pew Research Center, December 12,
     2019, https://www.pewresearch.org/short-reads/2019/12/12/u-s-children-
     more-likely-than-children-in-other-countries-to-live-with-just-one-
     parent/.
2.   Sara McLanahan, Laura Tach, and Daniel Schneider, "The Causal
     Effects of Father Absence," *Annual Review of Sociology* 39 (July
     2013), https://doi.org/10.1146/annurev-soc-071312-145704.

(Gen. 1:26). That he'd provide for us (John 14:2), laugh with us (Ps. 126:2–3), discipline us (Prov. 3:11–12), give us gifts (James 1:17), and save us from trouble (1 Pet. 1:3). And that he'd do this forever!

Those are enormous, gorgeous promises. Sometimes they're comforting, and sometimes they can seem too big to grasp—maybe even too big to do any good. What use is an eternal, unseen Father when my "check engine" light comes on? When I need somebody to check my math? When I need money?

Most of the time, fathering isn't about grand, sweeping gestures but about a regular, everyday, can-you-read-this-paper-for-me, can-you-drive-me-to-work, can-you-fix-my-phone relationship. What are the father-less supposed to do then?

"Do not worry," the Bible tells us over and over. "Your Father knows what you need before you ask him" (e.g., Matt. 6:8).

Let me testify to that. On a Monday afternoon, he's provided money when none was there before. On a Wednesday morning, he's brought conviction of sin. Over a weekend, he's given me laughter with friends. Every need—physical, emotional, spiritual, social—he sees. And like a good dad, he provides not what I want but what I need.

He's doing the same for you. Day after day, in the regular rhythms of life, God is fathering you—whether you have a dad or not.

RESPOND

Reflect on your relationship with your earthly father. What are you grateful for? How have you experienced God providing for, encouraging, disciplining, or rescuing you in the last few days?

Prince of Peace

KENDRA DAHL

READ

"For to us a child is born,
　　to us a son is given;
and the government shall be upon his shoulder,
　　and his name shall be called
. . . Prince of Peace." (Isa. 9:6)

REFLECT

There are many words I'd use to describe the Christmas season: joyful, hopeful, even magical. But not often peaceful. Festivities hijack my calendar while my to-do list grows to include the once-per-year tasks of house decorating, cookie baking, and gift shopping.

During the holidays, my propensity for conflict rises with my stress levels. I may enter the season envisioning peaceful moments spent in family worship beside the glowing Christmas tree, a fire crackling in the background. But my reality is more frazzled and frantic, with little margin to gather my family (and get the pets out of the Christmas tree) long enough to remember the reason for the season.

Christmas seems to surface a deep longing for peace in my home and my heart. But when I consider the world beyond my living room and the days filling my calendar long after the decorations are put away, I realize this longing is ever-present. We can't turn on the news without hearing of chaos, suffering, hostility, and strife. Wars big and small are waged around the world and, too frequently, around our kitchen tables. There's little we can do to bring about the peace we crave.

When Isaiah told God's people about the messianic King to come, the words "Prince of Peace" likely sent chills down their spines. World powers like Assyria and Babylon threatened Judah. But in the few verses prior, Isaiah told them they'd have reason to rejoice: deliverance was coming. In keeping with his promises, God's Messiah would break the rod of Israel's oppressor, easing his people's heavy burden (Isa. 9:4). The peace would be so complete that the soldier would no longer need his clothes and boots for war (v. 5).

Fixated on their national plight, the recipients of Isaiah's words saw in these promises the divided kingdom's union and the restoration of David and Solomon's glory days. But they may have missed the expansive, eternal nature of what the Messiah would accomplish for his people. The Prince of Peace would rule as the rightful heir to David's throne, but the peace he brings isn't temporary (v. 7).

Israel's greatest need wasn't deliverance from their earthly oppressors any more than our greatest need is the superficial quiet of contrived family moments and clear calendars or the circumstantial calm of ceasefires and resolutions. We don't need deliverance from our enemies; we *are* the enemies (Rom. 5:10). In our sin before God, we're children of wrath (Eph. 2:3)—"having no hope and without God in the world" (v. 12), "hated by others and hating one another" (Titus 3:3).

But the Prince of Peace was born in Bethlehem so we could have peace with God through him (Rom. 5:1). Christ himself is our peace, reconciling us to God and to one another through the cross (Eph. 2:14–16).

As the chaos of Christmas stirs our longing for peace, we can find rest in the peace Christ has secured. The Prince of Peace has come! And he has brought us near to God by his blood. In Christ, we receive an eternal peace that cannot be revoked or shaken, despite how unruly our circumstances may seem. And this peace of Christ rules in our hearts by his Spirit, equipping us for the peacemaking life of love that befits "God's chosen ones, holy and beloved" (Col. 3:12–17).

RESPOND

What circumstances in your life leave you longing for peace? How does recognizing Christ as the "Prince of Peace" provide comfort or hope?

PART IV

Good News Announced

Shepherds Abiding

WINFREE BRISLEY

READ

"In the same region there were shepherds out in the field, keeping watch over their flock by night. And an angel of the Lord appeared to them, and the glory of the Lord shone around them, and they were filled with great fear. And the angel said to them, 'Fear not, for behold, I bring you good news of great joy that will be for all the people.'" (Luke 2:8–10)

REFLECT

We tend to think we need special situations or experiences to hear from God. If we could just go on a retreat, find the right quiet-time journal, or practice a new spiritual discipline, maybe we'd really sense God's presence. Maybe he'd speak to us.

Retreats, resources, and spiritual disciplines can all be worthwhile. But it strikes me that when the angel appeared to the shepherds to announce Jesus's birth, they were going about their ordinary lives. They were out in the field, keeping watch over their sheep. The good news came to these men amid their ordinary faithfulness. I wonder if the same could be true for us.

Instead of assuming we have to get away from it all to be with the Lord, what if we went about our daily tasks remembering that Jesus came to earth and gave us his Holy Spirit? Because the Spirit indwells all who are in Christ, we're in God's presence wherever we are—on the highway and in the carpool line, at our kitchen tables and in our cubicles, on the sidelines and in the church pews. So how can we expect to hear from God's Spirit amid our daily lives?

Just as the angel pointed the shepherds to Jesus, so the Spirit is pointing us to the good news of Christ. But whereas the angel's announcement to the shepherds came with fanfare and stopped the hearers in their tracks, the Spirit speaks to us in a still, small voice we might easily miss—or be tempted to dismiss.

When he prompts us to sacrifice our interests to serve someone else, it may be easier to put our head down and check something off our to-do list. When he convicts us of sin and calls us to new obedience, it may be easier to turn on a podcast and continue business as usual. When he beckons us to spend time in his Word and prayer, it may be easier to pick up our phone and scroll. God speaks to us in these everyday moments. The question is whether we'll listen and respond.

Sometimes we have mountaintop experiences. Sometimes we sense the Lord's presence or direction with extraordinary nearness and clarity. But the Christian life isn't about seeking those moments. It's about abiding daily in the Lord and keeping watch over whomever or whatever he's entrusted to our care. It's about sitting under the teaching of God's Word and serving side by side with his saints. The good news comes to us right where we are.

If the monotony of life and the daily toil are wearing you down today, don't buy into the lie that you have to reach the top of the mountain to find joy in God's presence. Keep watch in the field. Keep abiding in the Lord. Wherever you are, hear the Holy Spirit say, "Fear not, for behold, I bring you good news of great joy."

RESPOND

What do you think hinders you from experiencing God's presence? How can you become more aware of the Holy Spirit's work and presence in your everyday life?

Angels Appear

ANDREW SPENCER

READ

"An angel of the Lord appeared to them, and the glory of the Lord shone around them, and they were filled with great fear. And the angel said to them, 'Fear not, for behold, I bring you good news of great joy that will be for all the people.'" (Luke 2:9–10)

REFLECT

An ominous envelope appeared in my mailbox one afternoon. It was official correspondence from the Internal Revenue Service. My heart fell as I started to read the letter inside. They'd found an error in my return and recalculated my taxes. *How much did I owe?* Thankfully, my concern over a looming bill turned to relief when I read I'd overpaid by about 30 dollars. The envelope contained a check. Sometimes good news comes in a scary package.

It's hard to imagine what it must be like to see an angel and glimpse God's glory. Isaiah had a vision of the throne room of God. He thought he'd die because God's glory was so bright (Isa. 6:5). When Moses soaked up the radiant glory of God, his face shone so brightly people wouldn't come near him (Ex. 34:30). At the transfiguration, Jesus shone with the glory of God and even his clothes were "intensely white," leaving Peter so overwhelmed he tried to worship Elijah and Moses (Mark 9:2–6). God's glory comes in a frightening package. It's little wonder the shepherds were flooded with fear when the angels showed up in a burst of glory.

Angels appear at significant moments in salvation history. Christ's birth was big news. Bigger than the protection of Lot and his family (Gen. 19:1). More important than the command to Jacob to return home (31:11–13). Certainly more significant than the calling of Gideon (Judg. 6:11–12). We usually read about angels visiting important people. Yet at just the right moment, in the fullness of time, some unsuspecting shepherds got a front-row seat for the announcement that the world had changed—God is with us.

Their gripping fear turned to overwhelming joy. The glory of God wasn't an announcement of their impending destruction. The message was that their guilt would soon be gone and their sins atoned for, similar to what Isaiah heard (Isa. 6:7). This time it wasn't through the purification of fire but through the promised Messiah's birth. The angelic visitation was a scarier package than an IRS envelope but an infinitely greater blessing. The flood of joy must have been overwhelming as the shepherds blinked in the light of God's glory. The rush of stress-induced cortisol turned to joy-soaked adrenaline.

This announcement of Christ's birth is much like our own moment of salvation. We may not have seen the visible glory of God, but we did experience his presence. In that moment, we recognized everything in our world had changed. We'd have to die, but we'd gain a life greater than we could imagine. Just like those shepherds who bounced from terror to joy, we too have been given an opportunity to revel in God's goodness and become heralds of salvation.

RESPOND

How does the shepherds' vision of God's glory remind you of the moment of your salvation? What keeps you from overflowing today with a sense of joy at the good news of Christ?

Born This Day

BENJAMIN L. GLADD

READ

"For unto you is born this day in the city of David a Savior, who is Christ the Lord. And this will be a sign for you: you will find a baby wrapped in swaddling cloths and lying in a manger." (Luke 2:11–12)

REFLECT

Luke 2 opens with one of the most familiar lines in the New Testament: "In those days a decree went out from Caesar Augustus" (v. 1). It's easy to gloss over this detail as we hear it read in Christmas plays and sermons year after year, but Luke includes it for a reason. He frames the birth of Christ within the reign of the mighty Caesar Augustus, who rules over one of the most powerful empires in world history. Luke wants his readers to see that Jesus's birth occurred under the thumb of the Roman government.

Then notice how Luke describes Jesus in verse 11: "Christ the Lord." The phrase can be translated as "The anointed one, the Lord." This is unusual, because we expect the often repeated phrase "anointed one *of* the Lord" that refers to Israel's kings (see 1 Sam. 24:6, 10; 26:9, 11). But here, the angel announces that Jesus is Israel's long-awaited Messiah *and* Lord. Jesus is both God and man.

As Caesar Augustus sits enthroned in his resplendent palace in Rome, Jesus, the true King, is born in the humblest of circumstances. He's "wrapped in swaddling cloths and lying in a manger" (Luke 2:12). One of Luke's central themes is the humiliation of the proud and the exaltation of the humble. As Mary remarks in the Magnificat, "[God] has brought down the mighty from their thrones and exalted those of humble estate" (1:52).

Jesus's entire life and ministry embodies unparalleled humiliation: he is born in the lowliest circumstances, serves those on society's fringes, and undeservingly bears God's wrath on his people's behalf. Yet on the cross, at Jesus's greatest point of humiliation, he unveils his identity as Israel's anointed King and Lord—the second person of the Trinity. Three days later, he rises from the dead and eventually ascends to the Father's throne—the highest position imaginable. Jesus's humiliation qualifies him to rule not just over Israel or the Roman empire but over the cosmos. How do we respond?

First, we adore Christ because of his humiliation and exaltation. God brought his Son unimaginably low on the cross and subsequently exalted him to the divine throne. Here we discover the depths of God's devotion to his people. What love! How often do we thank Christ for the riches of his boundless grace in this regard?

Second, we imitate Christ's humiliation and exaltation in our own lives. Of course, we'll never endure the same sort of humiliation and exaltation Christ experienced, but God calls us to "take up [our crosses] daily and follow" him (9:23). Our lives must be patterned after Christ's. We look for opportunities to humble ourselves and serve others. Especially during the Advent season, we're reminded to give of ourselves to others, but it should be our pattern all year long. And once we've spent our lives in service to each other, God promises to raise us and fashion us with new bodies fit for the new creation, where we'll rule with him for all eternity.

RESPOND

How does remembering Christ's humiliation and exaltation challenge you to humble yourself? What are practical ways you could serve others this Christmas and throughout the year?

Glory to God in the Highest

PHIL THOMPSON

READ

"Suddenly there was with the angel a multitude of the heavenly host praising God and saying,

> 'Glory to God in the highest,
>   and on earth peace among those with whom he is
> pleased!'" (Luke 2:13–14)

REFLECT

Peace. *Shalom*. Calm. Stillness. Balance. Rest.

My life feels unlike these words most days. The hustle to get kids out of bed and off to school isn't peaceful. The relentless stream of emails and text messages isn't calming. Juggling work and church and school and family feels anything but balanced. Rest doesn't come easy.

Peace feels like a far-off fantasy land where I don't have disagreements with my colleagues or where my kids get to bed without a fight or where my HOA settles down about the leaves in someone's yard or where the wars across the globe come to an end. Peace feels like nothing but a phantom, a mirage, an alternate reality.

But today's verses suggest peace can actually exist on earth. Is it possible this alternate reality of peace has broken in from another dimension? Has the most intangible hope of my life come home?

First, the angels tell us the source of peace—"Glory to God in the highest." Our problem is that we tend to reverse the angels' praise. We start with the problem: the need for peace in life, peace on earth. And then we go hunting for a solution to our needs. Eventually, we realize God is the solution. But the angels put praise in the primary place and our pains second.

You'll never have peace in your work so long as you put your problem-solving skills first and make prayer your backup plan. You'll never have peace with your extended family so long as you obsess about every argument you'll encounter over Christmas and forget the Holy Spirit's work. Peace only comes when we put God in his place first and foremost. *God, you reign over the pain in my life.*

Second, the angels tell us the place of peace—"And on earth peace." Here. Now. Peace has broken in. Peace has descended into the chaos of your home, your workplace, your school, your country. Believe it or not, peace has made its home with us. The unreal has become real. Can you believe it?

Third, the angels tell us the surprise of peace— "Among those with whom he is pleased." The final words of the praise chorus give us the shock of all shocks. The peace we long for and the peace that has come to earth isn't primarily for my home, my workplace, my school, and my country. It's a peace meant *for me*. It's a peace that comes to those who were at war with God and are now in a unique relationship with him. It comes to people he celebrates and dances over.

The angels speak to our greatest need in our chaotic, stress-filled, overworked, frantic, hair-on-fire lives. Peace . . . *with God*. What you need most isn't peace in your relationships with people but peace in your relationship with God. Only once you've found peace with God will you become a person of peace at the dinner table or the boardroom table.

RESPOND

What's your primary reaction when your world isn't at peace? Have you come to rest in the reality of the peace that Jesus offers between you and God? How can you take the peace of God into the world around you this Christmas?

PART V

Messiah
Believed

Rejoice Greatly, O Daughter of Zion

MATT SMETHURST

READ

"Rejoice greatly, O daughter of Zion!
    Shout aloud, O daughter of Jerusalem!
Behold, your king is coming to you;
    righteous and having salvation is he,
humble and mounted on a donkey,
    on a colt, the foal of a donkey." (Zech. 9:9)

REFLECT

Who is the most well-rounded person you know? For me, it's my brother-in-law Seth. The guy is good at things that typically don't go together. He's relational and he's analytical. He's a counselor and he's a mechanic. He's a mountain biker and a musician. Once, when my wife was pregnant, he knitted the unborn kid a hat. *The man knits.*

I could keep going, but you get the point. It's rare to find someone who combines seemingly opposite qualities. But Christmas is about the ultimate unexpected juxtaposition.

When we parachute into Zechariah 9:9, we land squarely in the soil of hope. The prophet is writing to returning Jewish exiles about their coming Messiah. This is the most famous verse in Zechariah's scroll because it's not the last time it appears in your Bible. Five hundred years later, the Gospel writers will note its fulfillment as one man enters Jerusalem for the last time.

Who is this man? He's the second person of the eternal Trinity, the Creator of the galaxies, the supreme Monarch of the universe, and the Lion of the tribe of Judah, for starters. Given such a résumé, we might expect him to enter the city in a show of messianic strength, perhaps on a chariot or a warhorse. Instead, we read that he comes "humble, and mounted on a donkey" (Matt. 21:5).

This is terribly inconvenient for visions of grandeur. Imagine the disciples the night before the triumphal entry. After they've spent days slogging toward Jerusalem, their Master says, "For the final stretch, I'm not going to walk in; I'm going to ride in." They begin pumping their fists, high-fiving, thinking, *Finally, he's talking like a king. Finally, he's going public. The Romans better take notice! Let's get him the biggest warhorse in the land.* His response? "Oh, I'm good. I've already reserved the smallest donkey you'll be able to find."

It's as unthinkable as the King of England riding into Buckingham Palace on a tricycle.

Jesus wasn't the kind of king they wanted, and he's not always the kind we want either. He bursts the banks of our expectations because his heart spills over with something we don't often associate with kingship: humility. To paraphrase one author, only in God's upside-down kingdom do messiahs ride donkeys and masters wash feet.

Jesus was the only person who ever deserved to strut. It would've been fitting for him to act entitled, to cling to his rights, to step on others to advance himself. But that never happened. The people he could have controlled, he served; those he could have used, he loved; those he could have shamed, he saved. Jesus Christ had every reason to strut, yet he limped. Meanwhile, we have every reason to limp, yet so often we strut.

In this world, weakness will often look like strength, and strength like weakness. The triumphal entry is a stark reminder that the Christian life will not always feel triumphant. Sometimes it'll be confusing. Sometimes it'll seem like you're staring at the back of a donkey—because that's what the King you follow has chosen to ride. Don't be enchanted by the pomp and circumstance of mere appearances.

When Julius Caesar entered Rome, he went to the temple of the pagan god Jupiter to offer sacrifices. But Jesus Christ entered Jerusalem to *become* the sacrifice for the sins of the world. And the great clue that his victory will burst our expectations is that there's no palace at his birth nor chariot as he rides to his death.

RESPOND

There's no greater threat to spiritual health than pride. Pride tempts us to strut, but true encounters with God result in limps (Gen. 32:22–32). In what ways are you clamoring for a chariot rather than following your expectation-defying King—born in a feeding trough, mounted on a donkey, stapled to a cross? How might his meekness, as both your Savior and your example, practically deflate self-absorption in your heart?

The Eyes of the Blind Shall Be Opened

ELLIOT CLARK

READ

"Then the eyes of the blind shall be opened,
    and the ears of the deaf unstopped;
then shall the lame man leap like a deer,
    and the tongue of the mute sing for joy.
For waters break forth in the wilderness,
    and streams in the desert." (Isa. 35:5–6)

REFLECT

In the opening of Mark's Gospel, he introduces us to the good news about Jesus Christ, the Son of God (1:1). His story begins in a peculiar place: the wilderness.

    Within the first 13 verses, Mark mentions "the wilderness" four times. The repetition is striking, especially in such a short section of Scripture. What's so significant about the wilderness?

While Mark records *what* happened, he also emphasizes *where* it happened. It's significant that Jesus (and John before him) appeared in the wilderness, because many Old Testament promises spoke of that place with hope.

According to Isaiah, the wilderness was where the Lord would one day return (Isa. 40:3). On that day, the wilderness would flow with water and become fertile (41:18). The curse of sin would be broken (43:25), and God's Spirit would be poured out in blessing on his people (44:3). The prophet was looking for the day when the wilderness would rejoice and be glad (35:1).

Isaiah 35 paints a striking picture of what to expect on that day. There will be refreshing streams rippling through the once-barren desert. The lame will leap. The mute will sing. The blind will see.

These promises aren't merely metaphorical or spiritual. For when Jesus arrives, he awakens Isaiah's sleeping prophecies. A paralyzed man springs to his feet (Mark 2:1–12). A deaf and mute man suddenly speaks (7:31–37). Perhaps most astonishing of all, the blind man sees (10:46–52).

In his classic work *On the Incarnation*, Athanasius reflects on the message of these miracles:

> He made the lame walk, He opened the ears of the deaf and the eyes of the blind, there was no sickness or weakness that He did not drive away. Even the most casual observer can see that these were acts of God. The healing of the man born blind, for instance,

who but the Father and Artificer of man, the Con-
troller of his whole being, could thus have restored
the faculty denied at birth? He Who did thus must
surely be Himself the Lord of birth.[1]

Jesus's power to open blind eyes compels us to see him
for who he truly is: the Maker of all. This too is a fulfillment of the prophet's words of hope for those in the wilderness: "They shall see the glory of the LORD" (Isa. 35:2).

During Advent, when we look on our Savior with
the eyes of faith, we recognize, with Athanasius, that the
baby in the manger is the Lord of birth. He's the One
who gives light to darkened eyes. He's the One who gives
life to the barren desert. Thus we're enabled by his Spirit
to heed the words of Isaiah 35:4: "Behold, your God."

RESPOND

Are you currently experiencing a season of dryness or
deadness? How does the incarnation, and Isaiah's promise of streams in the desert, give you hope? Do you have
eyes to see God's glory in the face of Jesus Christ?

1.   Athanasius, *On the Incarnation,* trans. John Behr (Crestwood, NY: St
Vladimir's Seminary Press, 1993), 47.

He Shall Feed His Flock like a Shepherd

MEGAN HILL

READ

"He will tend his flock like a shepherd;
    he will gather the lambs in his arms;
he will carry them in his bosom,
    and gently lead those that are with young."
(Isa. 40:11)

REFLECT

I'm not sure who thought it was a good idea to cast shepherds in a children's Christmas play. It's truly nothing short of madness to dress elementary-school boys in repurposed bathrobes, hand them wooden sticks, put them in charge of woolly preschoolers, and expect things to turn out well. Staffs *will* be used as swords and the sheep *will* cry. Little boys just don't make good shepherds.

Isaiah's hearers had experience with bad shepherds too. Over the course of Old Testament Israel's history, God's people had endured prophets and priests who failed to care well for them. Isaiah condemned religious leaders who should have fed and protected the flock of Israel but who instead "turned to their own way, each to his own gain" (56:11). Such shepherds were ignorant, lazy, greedy, selfish drunkards—and they harmed the sheep by their foolishness (56:9–57:1).

To people suffering under poor leaders, Isaiah's prophecy in today's verse would have been a glorious vision. Instead of the incompetent hirelings they'd had for generations, the Lord was going to send them a new shepherd. This shepherd would gather, rather than scatter, the sheep. He'd care for them rather than neglect them. He'd be gentle rather than abusive. This shepherd would lovingly do what their sinful leaders had failed to do. Best of all, this shepherd wouldn't simply be God's appointed servant. He'd be God himself (40:10).

For hundreds of years, God's people waited for this promise's fulfillment, and then, in John 10, Jesus made a bold statement: "I am the good shepherd" (v. 11). This was no mere agricultural metaphor. This was a declaration of Isaiah's prophecy fulfilled and of Jesus's identity as God. His followers would have knowingly received it with joy. Here, finally, was the Shepherd who'd nourish the sheep with his own body, quench their thirst with his own Spirit, defeat their enemies with his own wounds, and gather them safely to himself for eternity at the cost of his own blood.

Christ is the "great shepherd" (Heb. 13:20) and he's the "one shepherd" (John 10:16). He's the One whose voice we know and whose will we follow (v. 27). At times in this life, we may suffer under church leaders who fail us—sometimes grievously. We may have pastors and elders who neglect our souls or who sin against us. When we experience these griefs, we can cry out to the Lord as the people in Isaiah's day doubtless did, asking the Good Shepherd to care for us.

At other times, we'll have earthly shepherds who love and minister to us well, undershepherds who obey Christ the Chief Shepherd (1 Pet. 5:2). When we experience their faithful shepherding, we can give thanks. They're the gifts of the risen Christ to us (Eph. 4:10–12), and in their care we receive the care of Christ himself.

Whether you've experienced good or bad earthly shepherds, Isaiah's prophecy can remind you to trust in the Good Shepherd who promises to tend, gather, carry, and lead his sheep all the way home.

RESPOND

What needs do literal sheep have? How are those things a picture of believers' needs in the local church? In what ways does Christ tend, gather, carry, and lead the flock? Thank God for sending Jesus, the Good Shepherd, to care for you.

His Yoke Is Easy

IVAN MESA

READ

"Come to me, all who labor and are heavy laden, and I will give you rest. Take my yoke upon you, and learn from me, for I am gentle and lowly in heart, and you will find rest for your souls. For my yoke is easy, and my burden is light." (Matt. 11:28–30)

REFLECT

Christmas is my favorite time of the year, and yet it always disappoints. Even the sweetest moments are ephemeral: we say goodbye, we return to our jobs, we're reminded of loved ones no longer present, our kids grow up (and then leave), and the looming new year reminds us of past resolutions made and broken. The accumulation of disappointments, not to mention the busyness of the season, ends up leaving my soul weary. I somehow expect Christmas to give me the rest my heart yearns for. It never quite delivers.

For those, like me, who come to the end of a year worn and weary, the good news is that Christ offers us anew the gift of rest: "Come to me."

It must have been shocking to hear Jesus say he offered rest—both because it was a not-so-subtle claim to be God and because of the contrast with what the religious leaders of the day taught. After all, it was God who promised, "I will satisfy the weary soul, and every languishing soul I will replenish" (Jer. 31:25). Here Jesus offers rest in himself, the kind of rest only the God of the universe can give. And, unlike the scribes and Pharisees who imposed hard-to-bear, heavy burdens on people (Matt. 23:4), Christ promised his disciples an easy yoke.

Most days, I wake up already burdened. Whether because of the daily grind of life, indwelling sin that remains, or the reality of spiritual warfare, I rise each day in desperate need of God's fresh mercies. For others, it might be a prolonged season of suffering or a wayward child; it might be unfulfilled longings or the bitter taste of sin's consequences; it might just be the hustle and bustle of life that keeps us, like Martha of old, "anxious and troubled about many things" and devoid of Christ's "good portion" (Luke 10:41–42).

Wherever we are, we can find rest in Christ because he is our salvation. As much as we talk about knowing the gospel, sharing the gospel, and preaching the gospel to ourselves, it's important to remember we don't come to a thing called "the gospel." We come to a person. The good news of the gospel is that we get Christ. As John

Piper put it, "God is the gospel."[1] And if we get God, then we get what our souls were made for. Or as Augustine famously prayed, "You have made us for yourself, and our heart is restless until it rests in you."[2]

Our hearts were made to worship and know the one true living God. We were made to walk in fellowship with and dependence on his Word. Yet ever since the fall, we live in a restless world that seeks to fill that yearning with everything but God.[3] Even as Christians, we often experience the cares of this world luring our hearts away from the Lord (Mark 4:19). Amid all the voices that call for our attention, however, Christ's voice quietly pierces through with the same invitation today: "Come to me."

RESPOND

What burdens are you carrying this Christmas? In what areas of your life do feel restless? What might it look like for you to accept Christ's invitation and find your rest in him?

1. John Piper, *God Is the Gospel: Meditations on God's Love as the Gift of Himself* (Wheaton, IL: Crossway, 2005).

2. Augustine, *Confessions*, trans. Henry Chadwick, Oxford World's Classics (New York: Oxford University Press, 1992), 3.

3. See Benjamin Storey and Jenna Silber Storey, *Why We Are Restless: On the Modern Quest for Contentment*, New Forum Books 70 (Princeton, NJ: Princeton University Press, 2021).

Christmas Day

Hallelujah!

BRETT MCCRACKEN

READ

"Then I heard what seemed to be the voice of a great multitude, like the roar of many waters and like the sound of mighty peals of thunder, crying out,

'Hallelujah!
For the Lord our God
    the Almighty reigns.'" (Rev. 19:6)

"Then the seventh angel blew his trumpet, and there were loud voices in heaven, saying, 'The kingdom of the world has become the kingdom of our Lord and of his Christ, and he shall reign forever and ever.'" (Rev. 11:15)

REFLECT

When George Frideric Handel wrote the "Hallelujah" section to close out Part II of *Messiah*, he could hardly have foreseen how iconic the song would become. Nor could he have envisioned it'd inspire the most viral flash mob YouTube video of all time (not that he'd have fathomed words like "viral," "flash mob," and "YouTube").

You may have seen the video. Published in November 2010, it was recorded in Ontario's Seaway Mall food court by a local photography company. Eighty singers from the Chorus Niagara wore nondescript clothing, blending into their holiday shopping surroundings. Then one soprano, pretending to be on a phone call, daringly bursts into the first notes of the "Hallelujah" chorus. She's soon followed by fellow chorus members, standing as they join the song.

Onlookers—munching on their Arby's Beef 'N Cheddars and A&W Cheese Curds—appear stunned as their Christmas shopping excursion is momentarily infused with a goosebump-inducing encounter with the glory God is due. About a minute into the video, as the choir sings Revelation 19:6 ("For the Lord God omnipotent reigneth"), the look on one young boy's face is especially priceless. Wearing a Gap sweatshirt—behind him a sign for a $5 pizza special—the boy has a wide-eyed expression that sums up the transcendent power of the heavenly scene it pictures. The song stops us in our tracks and fixes our gaze on the stunning glory of Christ, the "King of kings and Lord of lords."

Handel seemed jolted by *Messiah* as he composed it. He often wept as he wrote, and on finishing the

"Hallelujah" section he purportedly told an assistant, "I did think I saw heaven open, and saw the very face of God."

It shows in the music. The heralding trumpets (the angel's instrument in Rev. 11:15), the thunderous timpani, the ascending sopranos as they take the "King of kings" refrain to stratospheric heights . . . It all adds up to a sublime work of musical art nearly unrivaled in its power to move people to tears and up off their seats.

Standing during the "Hallelujah" chorus is a tradition dating back to King George II, who (legend has it) was so moved during the London premiere that he stood in rapture, prompting the entire audience to follow suit. We stand as we sing it three centuries later—not because of any earthly king's example but because of the King of kings's boundless glory and white-hot holiness. And to think—this glorious King of the universe was once a frail baby in a Bethlehem manger and then an object of scorn on a Roman cross.

As we sing of this humble King to the rousing harmonies of Handel's masterpiece, we can't help but stand, close our eyes, lift our hands, and for a moment imagine ourselves as we'll one day be: among a multitude, "like the roar of many waters and like the sound of mighty peals of thunder," crying out a mighty chorus infinitely louder and grander than the greatest food court flash mob: "Hallelujah! For the Lord our God the Almighty reigns" (19:6).

RESPOND

Search on Google for "Christmas food court flash mob" and watch the video. Let the performance arrest you and lead you to joyful worship of Christ. As you go about your Christmas Day festivities, consider how you could carve out dedicated moments of singing worship. Individually or (even better) with others, join your voices with the "heavenly host" that was there at Christ's birth (Luke 2:13–14) and with the "great multitude" in John's vision (Rev. 19:6).

Scripture Index

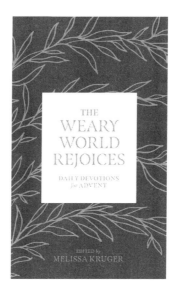

For generations, churches and families have used Advent wreaths to help prepare for celebrating the Lord's birth at Christmas. The evergreen wreath symbolizes eternal life and includes four candles—typically three purple and one pink, with a white candle in the middle that symbolizes the purity of Christ. Various traditions assign different topics to each candle, and the candles are usually given names to remind us of the good news of Christ's birth.

To celebrate this season, TGC's editorial team put together 25 devotional readings that use the Advent wreath as a guide to focus hearts and minds on Christ during the month of December. Structured around traditional Advent themes—hope, peace, joy, love, and faith—these reflections will encourage your heart in this season of celebrating Christ's first coming, and longing for his second.

ALSO AVAILABLE FROM THE GOSPEL COALITION

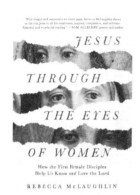

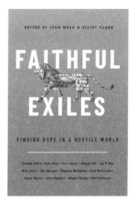

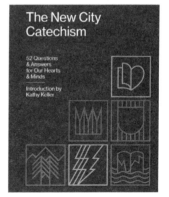